The Haunted Page and Otherworldly Oddities

Karan Bhasin

BookLeaf Publishing

India | USA | UK

Presentation by *BookLeaf Publishing*

Web: www.bookleafpub.com

E-mail: info@bookleafpub.com

ISBN: 9789360944315

First edition 2024

Broken Branches

Sway, sway the twisting arm,
Shadows creep and claw,
Hushed whispers draw terror of harm,
Beneath the willow etched with flaw.

When the wisps break,
And moonlight peeks down upon,
The sinister wood that wrings awake,
And calls for sinners ere next dawn.

Many moons before today,
When this wooden fright was yet small,
A town long forgotten lay,
The worst of us adorned its hall.

In rode justice one morn,
And a tree's branches grew and grew,
On the malice and the scorn,
Of the sinners and the last breath they drew.

The world moved on,
This tree stayed still,
Judge, jury all gone,
Yet executioner seeking thrill.

Now alone atop a sodden peak,
Reaching out and calling through the night,
For a mind and heart enough weak,
A chilling end to a chilling fright.

Pyre for the Fallen

There is a road not taken,
Left overgrown and unattended,
So those unaware are not mistaken,
And end up on this path unmended.

The folk around in hushed tones speak,
Of ghastly ghouls and unending marches,
Of a procession that may never break,
Cursed to pass from ashes to arches.

A foolhardy fellow once braved,
The road none other will take,
Dazzled by the lights, not one to be saved,
Drawn by the pyre over the lake.

The drums beat in time as the bodies burned,
A new soul to carry the tune,
A moment of regret for warning spurned,
The cleansing flame would take over soon.

Heaven's Lights

Life is fickle,
It will fade,
A slip up, a trickle,
And all is unmade.

One such soul wrought with fear,

Till the horns sound the invite,
"Ascend, ascend, our child so dear!"
One step, two step, all delight.

A quick look skywards,
Met with unfettered joy,
A sweeter song than the birds,
More mesmerizing than first love for a boy.

Eyes fixed on heaven's lights,
Each step an eternity with end in gaze,
A look down from dizzying heights,
Heat growing with heaven's lights ablaze.

A journey beyond life,
Is no place to be complacent,
For every step is bound to be rife,
With terror for the nascent.

But hearts will sing and flutter,
When on heaven's light they sip,
The question blinded by the clutter,
For this must be a one-way trip.

The veil lifted, the trance broken,
By an old face and a frown,
"From dark seduction you must be awoken,
If Heaven's light is up above, why do you climb
down?"

The Girl in the Window

There is an empty house in every town,
Unassuming but always there,
Some nights in the window a glimpse of a gown,
Most forget, some stop and stare.

Three hours past midnight,
The summer sun long gone,
The window shimmers in moonlight,
And a young boy's eyes are drawn.

A flash of a gown in the moonlight's flicker,
A silhouette now proud behind the window
frame,
The air around the boy slowly growing thicker,
"I want to play," with the wind the words came.

He could see her now, his mouth agape,
The girl in the window and her smile,
Captivated, the world around losing shape,
Maybe he will stay and play a while.

Many years pass, many boys forgotten,
And three hours pass midnight just in time,
For another boy begotten,
"Won't you stay and play?" Came the chime.

The boy looks up at that siren of glass,
As the shadows gather and grow,
It's too late for him, alas,
As he walks to the girl and the boy in the
window.

Bloodred Sandman

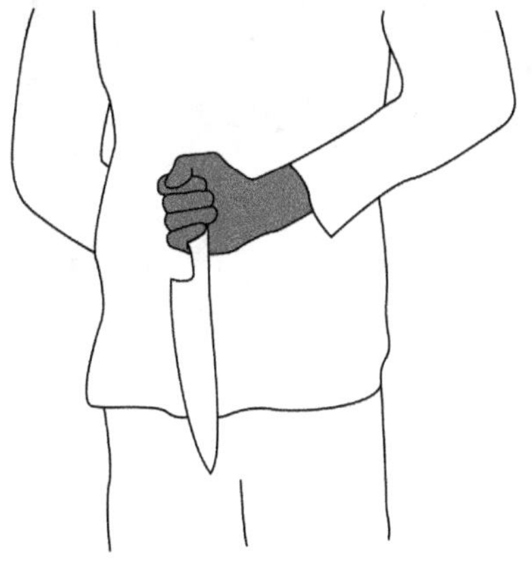

Pitter patter,
Run about, hide away,
Cut 'er, slash 'er,
Darkness will stay.

Plonkit, plankit,
Where did you go,
Bonk 'im, shank 'im,
Darkness will grow.

Star light, star bright,
Tears will flow red,
Shut your eyes tight,
Let sandman take you to bed.

Smile

I walk faster at night,
It's not that I'm in fear,
Of being away from the light,
Of the man behind me grinning ear to ear.

Nobody else sees him,
But he follows behind in the dark,
Just smiling his smile grim,
Broken eyes showing no spark.

He never gets closer,
But they say I should confront the smile,
That to find closure,
I should chat with my demon a while.

So I walk faster at night,
Because running away is easy,
Why stop and talk to my fright,
When my feet carry me breezy.

Yet they persist,
That I deal with what's in my mind,
Yet they insist,
That my cowardice is unkind.

So I walked slower last night,
And turned around and waved,
I'll bear that smile in my sight,
And give them what they craved.

I spoke to my demonic stalker,
In words I did not understand,
I continue to be a night walker,
The spring in my step still grand.

I still walk fast at night,
Don't look behind you,
Should you be out in twilight,
For now I smile too.

The Music

Starry-eyed visitor to traveling arts,
The clown, the juggler delighted,
As music grew and swelled in hearts.

Regaled by lights and carnival food,
And fire breather's flames ignited,
The music flowing alongside the mood.

Fixated on the majestic flames,
The slip of a hand or unhappy mind,
The music would cover all blames.

Fire burned, here and there,
The music a score too kind,
It burned and razed all bare.

The music played till it played no more,
The flames flicker out entwined,
No more laughter, no more lion's roar.

The music is just in my head,
It still rose and dipped,
The crowd around stayed dead.

The music won't play again,
Those roots had been snipped,
That was the end of it then.

A Leisurely Stroll

Beware the forests in summer time,
Through their unassuming tranquility,
And meditative chirp and chime,
Lay a wicked unseen facility.

They slumber in spring, fall and winter,
In summer raising their head,
From tree bark they begin to splinter,
For now comes the time for dread.

If you were to wander on a leisurely stroll,
A calming walk into that grotto of trees,
Past that bed of flowers, past that reaching knoll,
Feet lost to the wind, mind to the breeze.

You'll be in their home before long,
A string sounds a note in the air,
As you start to hear their song,
Bewitched now without care.

Branches twisting, warm embrace,
Calling out, ready to ensnare,
Binding you ever to this place,
So in summer time, of forests, beware.

The Deep Dark

Awake at last,
It's quiet, it's small,
Panic sets in fast,
When there isn't even space to crawl.

Barely able to move,
The thin air running out,
Help can not behooved,
When there's no one to hear you shout.

The sliver of light begins to fade,
No good to be worried,
Because what good is shade,
When before time you end up buried.

A sudden thud, a rapping steady,
To hear these noises so shocking,
But one must be ready,
When the deep dark comes knocking.

The House in the Rain

A freak storm,
A broken down car,
Only solace is a house forlorn,
Any other shelter would be too far.

The door slowly creaks,
For a house so old,
It's warm with no leaks,
Many secrets would this house hold.

A roof for the weary,
Is better than wicked rain,
So spooky and eerie,
That house that he could not explain.

He meant just to spend the night,
When the rain stops downpour,
He'll make his way without fright,
For now this house he will tour.

The twisting turning corridors,
His head felt light and bemused,
He spied through one of the doors,
An elixir surely meant to be consumed.

A wine this fine,
He had never had the joy,
Yet still a chill went down his spine,
For in the corner moved a toy.

"Child's play, a trick, a trick!"
He laughed, he chided,
"Hush now it'll just be a prick,"
An unseen voice confided.

The glass he cherished,
In his hand shattered,
And the flames of comfort perished,
A slight prick to his hand is all that mattered.

The Dance of Life

Two haunting lovers,
Danced atop the hill,
Through the flowers,
In the moon's spill.

Two beguiled dancers,
Where no one can spy,
The music of the stars spurs,
A magnificent lie.

For when a curious soul,
Draws nearer to the enthralled duo,
Smitten by the dance so droll,
The price of attendance too great to owe.

For no coin, no praise,
Can satiate the couple,
Who from graves did raise,
Only most precious will do for the dancers
supple.

The facade sinks,
Flesh was rotting, swaying and flaying,
A toothless grin, a wink,
The curious soul would be staying.

For artists must be paid,
And dancers must be fed,
It matters not now as he laid,
For soon he too would surely be dead.

Stay the Night

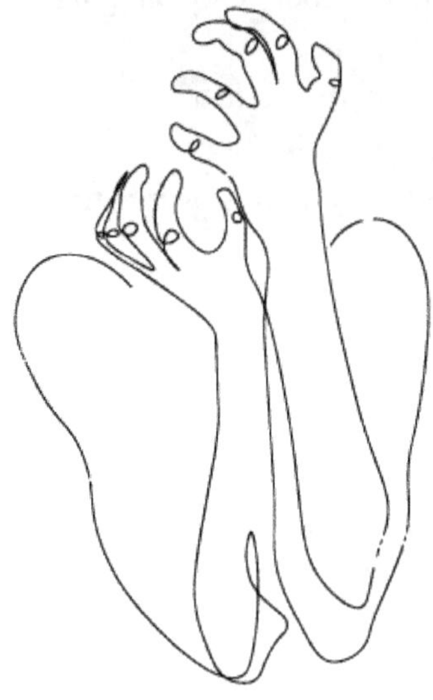

I do not like this place,
I would only stay the night,
And be gone come morning's trace.

It's moldy, it's rotten,
I would only stay the night,
In day time this will be forgotten.

The night is long, goes on and on,
I would only stay the night,
I can not bear the scorn.

The walls they are judging,
I would only stay the night,
For till light the door is not budging.

I've recently started to fear,
I would only stay the night,
But the night never ends over here.

Thirteen

"The thirteenth month will bear,
The thirteenth son of salvation."
The words they were clear,
"Will save this damned nation."

He pondered, he thought,
But there's no more year after December,
Maybe their notes hold what he sought,
But of the guild he's no longer a member.

The damned masses weighed his heart,
The world did need saving,
To give them a new start,
Was his one last craving.

So he broke in with good intention,
And looked for answers and hope,
And find he did a book that did mention,
He'd need sage and a length of rope.

Trinkets, herbs and one disgrace,
He'd need innocent blood,
A small price to pay, a stoic face,
And his doted son fell with a thud.

The price was paid to save all in sight,
The spell goes awry, somethings amiss,
As the clock strikes midnight,
And December gives way to the abyss.

Stir Not the Hunter

Stir not the hunter,
Watching over the creek,
For the hunter hunts for the meek,
The huddled, the soft and the weak.

Stir not the hunter,
So his aim may stay true,
As his eyes stay fixed on the blue,
From tiger to bison, even a shrew.

Stir not the hunter,
Never look him in the eyes,
For no matter how hard he tries,
He cannot hide all lies.

Stir not the hunter,
Forever he will stay,
And do not try to send him away,
Lest you become his prey.

The Haunted Page

The power of the word,
Can move even the stiffest foe,
Whether read or heard,
Ideas they can grow.

And ideas become belief,
That shape the world around,
Words long, words brief,
Can amaze and can astound.

Words will evoke emotion from stone,
You'll laugh, you'll smile, you'll cry,
You'll be chilled to the bone,
The words wouldn't even have to try.

They can build empires,
They can fell lives,
Deep rooted, a word never expires,
A word now it always survives.

But words are cold and unfeeling,
They are given their power with forethought,
Not always are words for healing,
In words the power of all ruin is wrought.

So what happens when words are evil,
When they inspire wickedness instead,
When words bring undue upheaval,
When they fill up with sorrow and dread.

A glorious tool corrupted,
With malice and anger the writing,
A dam of darkness erupted,
And in every mind now writhing.

Thoughts of the ghastly,
Can bring life to that which should not be,
An imagination that so vastly,
Spans and encompasses all that is free.

Words written on the haunted page,
Give worth to an untamed eternity,
Filled with sorrow, filled with rage,
Making unholy doom a certainty.

The Shop With No Sign

There is a hopeful destination,
For those at their bleakest,
They'll find this unseemly apparition,
That finds its way to the weakest.

Should you spy it turn away,
Even if it looks like any other,
Inviting as it may be to the stray,
There's always a choice, pick 'nother.

For in this shop you will find,
Everything you did ever seek,
But please pay mind,
The prices will make you meek.

No card, no credit, no cash,
No upfront payment is asked,
It'll be done and delivered in a flash,
And you'll forget till your time is tasked.

Ten years from the day,
You got all you desired,
A gentle humming will begin and stay,
And mind will turn to when all was acquired.

Was that shop seen once more,
Not at all, it may have been a dream,
But now that the bill stands before,
All that's left to do is scream.

Rest Now Little One

Rest now little one,
Time for play is done,
Let sleep take charge,
For now is time for a dreamy sparge.

Rest now little one,
Time for play is done,
Fret not the sounds,
Or the howling of hounds.

Rest now little one,
Time for play is done,
Should the bed shake,
Be sure you're not awake.

Rest now little one,
Time for play is done,
For we are in their domain,
All they revel in is the insane.

Rest now little one,
Time for play is done,
Should you open those unsullied eyes,
I hope, I hope I do not hear your cries.

The Lone Shipman

Fifty nights and fifty days,
Sailed the good ship far away,
And bore with it a man so pale,
Or so goes that melancholic tale.

A lad of bright standing,
He sought passage to the landing,
But the sea has notions of its own,
Waves were tossed, the ship thrown,

One by one they all disappeared,
Into swirling depths which they afeared,
Shores a distant memory,
Even further than shared revelry.

The waves crashed and they took,
As the ship hull it shook,
All but one bright eyed lad,
With little reason left to be glad.

The seas took him where they pleased,
He begged, he cried, he wheezed,
But no answer, no mercy,
The lone shipman pursy.

He wished he'd see again,
The faces he tried to recall in vain,
But the sea is all he knows now,
No more balls or dinners highbrow.

Every so often he'd look down below,
Aware there's only one way to know,
Eyes wide and a deep breath,
He puts one foot ahead.

The ship now sails the lonely water,
Shuddering, sighing, barely a totter,
The last soul in its grace,
Elected instead for a watery embrace.

www.ingramcontent.com/pod-product-compliance
Lightning Source LLC
LaVergne TN
LVHW010836200726

843508LV00012B/2620